# Too Many Visitors
# for One Little House

story by Susan Chodakiewitz   •   illustrations by Veronica Walsh

A Booksicals Children's Book

# Booksicals

Encouraging the sweetness of reading

## www.booksicals.com

· · · · · · · · · · · · · · · · · · · · · · · · · · · · · · · · · ·

ISBN: 1-4196-5470-5
ISBN-13: 9781419654701
Library of Congress Control Number: 2008904791

Summary: The story of three crabby neighbors, a new family on the block, a big family reunion, and the importance of being included.
1. Family - fiction  2. Kids  3. Neighbors  4. Pets  5. Family Reunions  7. Being Included  8. Visitors
9. Visiting Family  10. Family Holiday  11. Feeling Left-Out

The text of this book is set in Qlassik and Savoye LET fonts.

Illustrations are hand-drawn with digital color.

Printed in the United States by Booksurge.

Booksicals, a division of State of the Art – *Bringing stories to life*
www.storiestolife.com

# For my family:

Moocles, Sefi, Kalman, Meir, Tali, cousins Candice, Lauren, Jackie, Danielle, Gershon, Zina and Leora, Aunt Annie, Aunt Liba, Uncle Dale, Great-Uncle Isaac, Grandma, Grandpa, Bubbie, and Meeskite the-scraggly-dog – who all stayed at our house one not-so-quiet summer.

And thanks, PZ Miller, for your constant encouragement and guidance

The neighbors of El Camino Street did *not* like pets. They did *not* like kids. They did *not* like people with big families. They never had any guests and spent their day cleaning their houses, tending their gardens, and snoozing on their porches.

When the new family on the block moved in—a mom, a dad, three kids, and a fish—the neighbors kept an eye out for trouble. Yet life remained as usual...until the day the visitors arrived.

Welcome

We're on our way! Can't wait to see you! love, Grandma and Grandpa

First, the biggest camper they ever saw pulled up.

It took up half the block.

Before the engine stopped, out hopped
the teenage cousins:

a fancy teen in heels, dragging hangers filled
with clothes; a plugged-in teen with headphones,
waving teen magazines; and a zippy teen on
skates, holding soccer balls and skateboards.

The neighbors shook their heads and said,

"Too many visitors

for one **little** house!"

Now out came the grown-ups and a toddler:
a travel-weary aunt, dragging loads of smelly laundry;
a take-it-easy uncle, holding one light pillow; and a
sticky-licky toddler, hugging twin stuffed monkeys.

The toddler offered the neighbors one of her monkeys

The neighbors shook their heads and said,

**"Too many visitors
for one little house!"**

Then out of the camper door came a cane.
Attached to the cane was a hand. Grandma came
out, clutching bottles of prune juice. Grandpa brought
a plunger and rolls and rolls of toilet paper.

The neighbors shook their heads and said,

"Too many visitors
            for one **little** house!"

Then from inside the camper came a voice.
Attached to the voice was Nanny. Nanny rolled
out in a daredevil wheelchair. "Here I come," said
Nanny, "with some fresh apple strudel!"

The neighbors shook their heads and said,

**"Too many visitors for one little house!"**

The neighbors tried their hardest *not* to whiff
Nanny's delicious apple strudel.

Now a pair of boots stepped out. Attached to the
boots was—"Surprise!"— another uncle. He brought
fat babushka dolls all the way from Russia. Inside
each babushka, there were more babushka dolls!

All those babushkas blocked the neighbors' view.

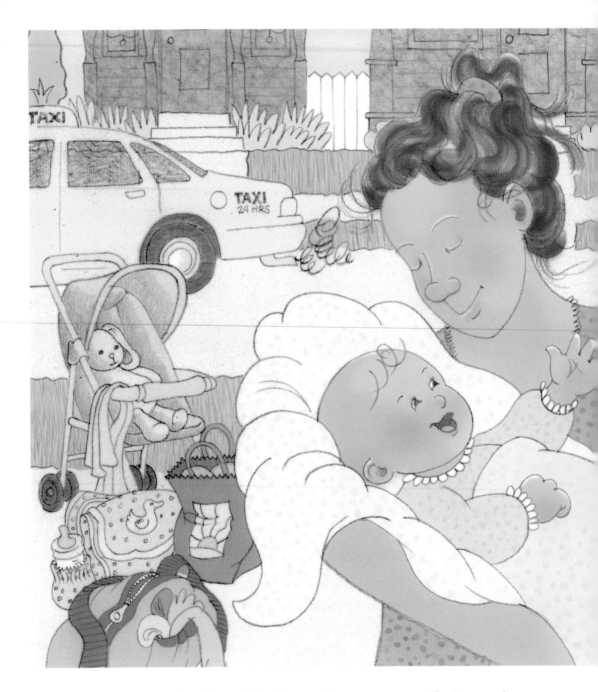

Now a taxicab pulled up. From out of the cab came a blanket. Snug in the blanket was a baby. Holding the baby was the family's married daughter. The rosy little baby flashed her biggest toothless smile.

The neighbors tried their hardest not to coochy-coo the rosy baby. They *hated* babies.

In the living room, cousins hugged and cousins kissed, and uncles and aunts pinched cheeks. The neighbors had never seen so many huggy-kissy people. They *hated* huggy- kissy families.

The neighbors shook their heads and said,

**"Too many visitors for one little house!"**

Then in the kitchen, dishes clattered and glasses clinked. Teapots whistled. Laughter roared.

The kids plugged in their electric guitars. Grandpa joined in with his clarinet.

The neighbors tried their hardest not to boogey to the beat. They *hated* music.

Now a scraggly dog came by. He stopped in front of the house.

Into the house wagged the dog, following the scent of Nanny's strudel.

Up went his tail to the lively rock 'n roll. "Woof!" barked the dog. He had finally found a home.

The neighbors had seen *all* the family activity they could bear!

*Something* had to be done.

They held a meeting.

Just as they were heading out to the city's complaint department...

Out of the house came the mom, holding a tray of apple strudel.

"Won't you join
              our **little** family reunion?"

the mom asked the neighbors.

The neighbors smiled and happily said:

"There are never too many visitors for one **little** house!"

Go to www.booksicals.com to:

- ORDER a copy of Too Many Visitors for One Little House

- VISIT with the family and neighbors on El Camino Street

- Get Nanny's strudel recipe and more...

- LEARN about Booksicals' performances and upcoming books

- ALSO available at Amazon.com

3817407